Generation Ship

George Ivanoff

Illustrated by Martin Bailey

KINGSCOURT / McGRAW-HILL

Generation Ship
Copyright © 2001 Rigby Heinemann

Rigby is part of Harcourt Education, a division of
Reed International Books Australia Pty Ltd ABN 70 001 002 357.

Text by George Ivanoff
Illustrations by Martin Bailey
Designed by Andrew Cunningham

KINGSCOURT/McGRAW-HILL

Shoppenhangers Road, Maidenhead
Berkshire, SL6 2QL
Telephone: 01628 502730
Fax: 01628 635895

www.kingscourt.co.uk
E-mail: enquiries@kingscourt.co.uk

Printed in Australia by Advance Press

10 9 8 7 6 5 4 3 2 1

ISBN: 0-07-710326-2

Contents

DEDICATION

This book is for Henry Callum Tully Gibbens,
one of the newest generation.

Prologue

"…and I salute all the brave people who have been chosen to go on this historic voyage in search of a habitable planet."

The family were gathered in the lounge-room watching the United Nations President on the holo-viewer, just like millions of other people all over the solar system.

"How long will it take?" asked the boy.

"No-one really knows," his older sister answered. "That's why they've got plants and animals on the spaceships."

"Okay, quiet everybody," their father interrupted. "We're getting to the interesting bit."

They looked at the President's holo-image.

"It is now my humble honour to officially launch human-kind's first real step beyond this solar system and into the greater universe."

The President's image faded and was replaced by five giant spaceships, stationary, just beyond Pluto. Then with a blinding flash, the engines ignited.

"Wow!" exclaimed the boy, as he watched Earth's first inter-stellar colonists leave on their long journey into the unknown.

CHAPTER ONE

The Nat World

JARDEEN RAN. He ran through the pine forest until he was out of breath. He ran until he could run no more. Finally, he collapsed to the ground, closing his eyes, the pine needles forming a soft bed to lie on.

Stupid kids, he thought. What do they know anyway?

As he lay there with his eyes closed, trying to regain his breath, Jardeen decided that he would have to learn to keep his opinions to himself. And he would have to learn not to take things so personally. I mean, it was silly really—now wasn't it? Running off like that.

And just because of a little argument. Well, it wasn't really little. There were four of them and only one of him. Jardeen sighed. He shouldn't have argued. But they were wrong.

Jardeen sighed again and opened his eyes. He looked up through the trees to the pale glow above. The soft, colourless light always fascinated him—or rather, it was the possible alternatives that fascinated him. He would often look up and wonder what a real sky would look like. He had seen pictures of Earth in books, but had never seen the Sun for himself. He wondered what it would be like, when he finally did see a real sky with a real Sun.

As his breathing returned to normal, Jardeen sat up. Looking around, he realised that he didn't recognise his surroundings. The trees were closer together and the only other plant life was an occasional fern. Obviously, he had run a lot further than he first thought.

Jardeen liked going into the pine forest, even though he wasn't supposed to. No-one ever ventured into the forest—except the Elders, of course. Sometimes, they would follow the road through the centre of the forest to meet the Tech leaders.

Well, he decided, getting to his feet, since I'm here, I might as well have a look.

As he walked, Jardeen looked all around, observing everything—different plants, birds, the occasional rabbit that came hopping past, and the slight breeze. Sometimes, when he was looking at his surroundings like this, he had to remind himself that he was on a spaceship, not a planet.

He stopped for a moment to feel the cool breeze on his face.

It must be lunchtime, he thought. The breeze always began at noon. Deciding he wasn't really hungry, he pressed on. Just a little further.

As he walked, he continued to think about the spaceship. He often thought the fact that the weather was always the same would be enough to convince the other kids they weren't on a planet. According to the books, weather on Earth was very unpredictable. But here on the ship it was always so ordered.

During summer, it was always pleasantly warm, never too hot so that the crops died, and there would be a cool breeze from noon till four, and rain from midnight till two. The other seasons were just as ordered. Never too hot, never too cold. Never too dry, never too wet. Always perfect. It just couldn't be real. Jardeen thought, that over the generations, people aboard the ship had simply forgotten what real weather was like.

Jardeen still couldn't understand why the grown-ups allowed the kids to think they were on a planet. His parents knew they were aboard a spaceship; he'd heard them talk about it, but they never corrected his sister, Nala. She'd rave on about how it was the Techs who'd made up the whole spaceship story to keep the Nats in their place, to stop them from going into Tech territory, but his mum and dad never argued. Nala would spend hours with her friends, talking about the lie, as she called it.

Suddenly, Jardeen glimpsed something in the distance. He walked a little further. It was large and grey. As the trees began to thin out, he finally realised what it was—a wall. A huge, grey metal wall.

Jardeen ran the rest of the way towards it. He looked up. It rose up quite a distance and then just seemed to meld into the glow. He looked to one side, and then the other. The wall stretched on for kilometres before curving out of sight beyond the trees.

"Wow!"

This is it, he thought. This is the end of our world and the beginning of the next.

Jardeen had heard many stories about the Dividing Wall which separated the Nat world from the Tech world. He'd always wanted to see the wall for himself.

He reached out his hand to touch it.

"Hello!"

Jardeen nearly jumped out of his skin. There should not have been anyone else around. But when he turned, there she was. Jardeen had seen Techs before, on their regular visits to trade goods with the Elders, but he had never seen one up close. She wore a dark blue uniform, just like those who came to their village, and a bracelet on her left wrist, with a shiny metal disk dangling from it. She was shorter than Jardeen, but he was quite tall for his age. Her hair was dark and her skin pale. He thought it was an odd contrast, but her smile and sparkling eyes made her look beautiful.

"You're a Nat, aren't you?"

Jardeen nodded hesitantly, still staring at her. "And...you're a Tech?"

She nodded. The two of them stood in silence for a while, looking each other over. Her hair was only shoulder length, which Jardeen thought looked strange. All the Nats had long hair. I wonder if she thinks I look strange, thought Jardeen, raising a hand to his long ponytail.

Finally, the Tech girl took a deep breath and came a few steps closer.

"My name's Tria," she said.

"I'm Jardeen." He held out his hand to her, carefully.

She came forward and shook it. "Pleased to meet you."

"Ah, yeah." Jardeen was finding it hard to hide his surprise. "What are you doing here?"

"Oh, just looking around." She took a little walk in a circle, looking this way and that, coming to a stop beside one of the pines. "I've never seen real trees before." She reached out and placed both her hands on the trunk.

"Really?" Jardeen was shocked.

Tria smiled. "Really!"

"Don't you have trees where you come from?"

Tria shook her head sadly, taking her hands off the pine. "No trees. No plants. No animals. Just machines."

"Oh!"

"I've seen pictures and holo-vids, but I wanted to see some real ones. How can you be expected to explore a planet's surface if you've never seen real plants and animals before?"

"Explore a planet's surface?"

"Oh, that's right," she said, turning away.

"You people don't believe we'll ever find a planet."

"Yes. Yes I do," stammered Jardeen. "I do believe we'll find a planet. At least, I hope we will. I think about it every day. What it will be like to see a real sky, a real sun..."

Tria turned to face him again and grinned. "Me too!" The excitement was plain on her face. "That's what I've been training for. That's why I've come here. This is about as close to it as I'll get till we actually find a planet." She spread her arms and waved them about. "You're so lucky to live among all this."

"Me. Lucky?" Jardeen didn't understand. "You're the lucky one. You know what's going on. I'm living with people who don't think we'll ever find a planet. Most of the kids don't even believe we're on a spaceship."

"Really?"

"Yes, really!" Jardeen looked into her eyes. "But your people believe. And they're preparing for it... aren't they?"

Tria nodded.

"Tell me about it?" asked Jardeen. "Please."

"Okay," agreed Tria. "But first, let's have something to eat. I'm starving."

She plonked down under one of the trees and rummaged through a pouch on her belt.

"Here we are," she said, pulling out a small box.

"What's that?" Jardeen asked, sitting down beside her.

"Lunch, of course." Inside the box were several sticks of something brown. It looked like they were made of clay, thought Jardeen.

Tria handed one to him, then took one herself and started chewing on it. Jardeen sniffed at it cautiously.

"Don't you have a sandwich?"

"What's that?"

"Never mind." He stared down at the little brown stick.

"It's okay," laughed Tria. "It's a nutrition stick. Go ahead and eat it."

Jardeen took a small bite and chewed. It had a strange flavour that he didn't recognise, but it was not unpleasant. He took another bite.

"Okay," said Tria, swallowing the last of her lunch, "what do you want to know?"

Jardeen looked up at her between bites, excitement sparkling in his eyes. "What's it like in your world? How did you get through the wall? When are we going to land on a planet? Everything!"

🕸 🕸 🕸

Nareen strode out of the barn and stopped at the edge of the cornfield. He looked around as if searching for something.

Nareen was a big man—tall and muscular. Like most Nat men, he had a beard and long hair tied neatly back out of the way. While his hair was jet-black, his neatly trimmed beard was dotted with grey. He sighed. A farm-hand had been injured while chopping wood and his son had disappeared when there were chores to be done.

"What am I going to do with that boy?" he asked himself in frustration.

Jardeen was always off somewhere. He was probably exploring the pine forest, which he shouldn't be doing. That boy always had his head in the clouds, talking about planets and starting a new world. There wasn't going to be any new world. This was it—the sooner he accepted that, the better things would be.

Nareen shook his head slowly and walked back to the barn. He would have to talk to Jardeen.

✦ ✦ ✦

Jardeen watched as Tria pressed her hand up against the metal plate on the wall. It slid back to reveal several rows of buttons, each with a number or a symbol. She pressed a series of the buttons and a section of the wall slid away to reveal a doorway.

"Wow!" Jardeen stared in amazement. "That's where you live?"

"Yep," Tria replied. "Now I better go before I get into trouble."

Suddenly there was an electronic buzzing sound.

"Too late," she sighed, fishing a small box-like device from her pouch.

"Where are you?" boomed an angry voice from the box.

"Um…"

"You have gone through the wall. You know that's against the rules. You think just because your mother…"

Tria switched it off and the voice stopped.

She looked up at Jardeen's stunned expression.

"Ah, that was Marshal Atrec, our Chief of Security. I'd better go."

She went through the doorway, then looked back at Jardeen.

"Don't worry," she smiled. "His bark is worse than his bite."

Jardeen wasn't convinced. He shivered at the thought of the cold, angry voice. Then the door slid shut.

🕸 🕸 🕸

"Hello," Nareen's wife, Gwenna, greeted him as he walked into the kitchen. She was as tall as her husband, with long blonde hair. Like him, she wore the standard grey coveralls that most Nats wore. "How was your day?"

"I've had better," he grunted.

Gwenna just smiled and started to set the table. She had discovered long ago that when her husband was in a bad mood, the best thing to do was to ignore it and act as if everything was fine. If she kept that up, Nareen would soon find it difficult to stay in a bad mood.

"Where are Nala and Jardeen?"

"Nala's in the village with her friends." Nareen met his wife's eyes. "As for that boy, your guess is as—" Nareen stopped when he heard the front door open.

"Jardeen," he shouted. "In here! Now!"

"Hi," said Jardeen, poking his head in the kitchen door. "I'm not late for dinner, am I?"

"No, you're not," said his mother.

"Dinner is not the issue," his father said sternly. "Your where-abouts is the issue. Off exploring, no doubt, in places where you're not supposed to go. Garant was injured today and then you run off instead of doing your chores."

"Sorry," said Jardeen.

"Sorry isn't good enough." His father looked directly at him, staring him down. "Tomorrow you'll be doing more than just your allotted chores—you'll be putting in a full day's work on the farm." He raised his hand to stop any potential protest from Jardeen.

Jardeen sighed. Not because he was going to be working all day tomorrow—he was expecting that. He sighed because his head was spinning with all the things that Tria had told him about. He so desperately wanted to tell someone, but knew he couldn't. He sat at the table and silently ate his dinner, while his mind ran through all the amazing possibilities.

🕸 🕸 🕸

Lying in bed that night, Jardeen listened to the distant, muffled voices of his parents.

"He'll grow out of it, Nareen," said his mother.

"I hope so," said his father.

"You worry too much."

"Perhaps I do. It's just that if he keeps dreaming about what he can't have, he'll never settle down and be happy with what he does have. I really do wish he was more like other kids."

"Nareen? Really?"

"What I mean is, I think he'd be better off if he didn't know we were aboard a ship. Most kids these days don't believe in the spaceship. They just think it's a fairy tale and they're better off for it. They're happy with their lives the way they are. They don't keep dreaming of something more."

"Oh," she said quietly. "Is that really what you think?"

"Sometimes I think we made a mistake in giving him access to all those books."

"You mean you think *I* made a mistake. It was me who encouraged his interest."

Then there was silence. There were some muffled sounds of movement for a while, and then he heard their bedroom door close.

Jardeen stared up at the ceiling. Was it so wrong for him to dream of finding a planet? Was he wrong in wanting to learn more about the ship in which they lived?

Meeting Tria today had confirmed all he had hoped and dreamed of. It had opened up a whole new world of possibilities. She and her people believed in the truth—that they were aboard a ship; that they were going to find and colonise a planet.

They were preparing for that day, teaching and training their children. Not like his people, who just lived their dull lives from day-to-day, thinking no further than their daily routines.

Jardeen was still awake when his sister came home. He heard the front door open and footsteps in the hall. Nala was always spending time in the village with her friends and coming home late.

It's not fair, he thought. She never gets into trouble.

True to his word, Jardeen's father made sure that he had lots of work to do the following day—everything from mending the scarecrows in the corn field to sweeping out the hen house. It was not until just before dinner, that Jardeen was able to have a moment to

himself. His father had gone off to do something else, so Jardeen took a few moments to sit down on the bench just outside their farmhouse.

In the distance, he could see Nala with some of her friends. They had come over for a visit, as they often did, and had spent the afternoon out by the edge of the corn-field engaged in deep discussions. Jardeen had heard bits of their conversation while mending a scarecrow.

"We're like slaves to the Techs," said one of them.

"Yeah," agreed another. "They give us bits of machinery, but we have to give them the stuff we grow."

Then, after some angry murmuring, he heard Nala say, "It won't always be like this."

Now, as Jardeen watched, her two friends got on their bicycles and headed off. Nala started walking in his direction.

"In trouble again," she teased as she approached.

Jardeen shrugged his shoulders. Nala was almost five years his senior. At eighteen years of age, she enjoyed a lot more freedom than he did. When they had been younger, it had seemed like her only purpose in life was to torment him. But over the last couple of years she had been changing.

She hardly spoke to him these days. She spent less time on the farm and a lot more time with her friends in the village. She talked a lot about how unfair things were between the Nats and the Techs. She didn't believe they were aboard a ship; in fact, she fervently believed the whole story had been made up by the Techs.

"Have you been out exploring?" she asked.

Jardeen nodded and walked over to Nala. She was a little shorter than him, with blonde hair like their mother. Her eyes constantly darted around, rarely meeting his.

"In the pine forest?"

Jardeen nodded again. This was a bit strange. Nala didn't usually take this much interest in him.

"You've been in the forest a few times," she said casually. "What's it like?"

"Lots of trees," Jardeen answered.

"I'm sure." Nala smiled. "I've heard stories about a wall. A big wall beyond the trees."

Jardeen looked down, not saying anything.

"You've been there, haven't you?"

"Maybe."

"Tell me about it." She put a hand on his shoulder. "I promise I won't tell on you."

Jardeen looked up at her. Was she really interested?

"Go on," she insisted. "Please!"

Suddenly, Jardeen was telling her about the wall and Tria and everything she had said. Nala listened intently and asked many questions.

That night, Jardeen didn't sleep much. He was too excited. After having spoken to Nala, he had decided that he just couldn't stay on the farm knowing what he knew. He had to follow his dream.

Early the next morning, much earlier than his parents usually awoke, he got out of bed. Leaving a note on the kitchen table, he stuffed a couple of biscuits in his mouth, grabbed his bag and headed out towards the pine forest.

Unseen by Jardeen, Nala peered through her bedroom window as he walked away from the farm. After he was out of sight, she went to kitchen and found the note. She read it, smiled and then used it to kindle the fire.

CHAPTER TWO

The Tech World

JARDEEN PRESSED his hand against the panel and it slid away. Then he pressed the same buttons Tria had pressed when she left. He stood silently as the doorway appeared—the doorway into another world. Through it, Jardeen could see a grey metal corridor.

Heart pounding, Jardeen took a deep breath and walked inside. He stopped and looked around. Grey metal—that's all there was. Grey metal walls and ceiling that stretched on ahead of him. The bird-song and rustling sounds of the forest had been replaced by a low humming—so quiet he almost didn't notice it. It was nothing like what he expected. He had thought there would be people, maybe even Tria, waiting to meet him. A silly expectation, he realised as he took another step.

Suddenly, the air was filled with a deafening noise, a kind of electronic wailing, and lights began to flash red. He turned around just in time to see the door slide shut.

Jardeen was being marched down grey metal corridor after grey metal corridor. One man in a black uniform walked beside him, another followed behind. Leading the way was a woman, also in a black uniform, but with blue markings along her collar and sleeves. She seemed to be in charge.

They stopped in front of a grey metal door. The woman pressed her palm to the panel beside the door, and a voice said, "Yes?"

"We have the intruder," she said, then looked back at Jardeen. "Ah…he's a child."

"Bring him in." Jardeen shivered at the cold voice. It sounded like Atrec.

The door slid open silently and Jardeen was led into a room, which had grey metal walls. It was a fairly small room with a large desk—also grey, also metal. Behind the desk sat a stern looking man. Jardeen breathed a sigh of relief upon seeing him. For a moment, he had the unreasonable thought that whoever sat behind this desk in this room at the end of all the corridors, might in fact be made of grey metal, too. But he wasn't. He looked as human as any Nat.

The man was tapping away at a series of

letters and numbers on the top of his desk. Above the desk, words and sentences floated in the air, new letters and numbers appearing as the man tapped away.

"Dismissed," he said without looking up. "And you can put your bag down if you want."

The woman and two men left silently, the door sliding shut behind them. Jardeen placed his bag on the floor.

The man kept tapping away. He was bald, with a long nose and small beady eyes. He did not look at all happy. After a few minutes more, he stopped.

"Complete," he announced. The sentences vanished, as did all the numbers and letters on his desk, leaving a clean surface.

"So you're a Nat?" he said finally, looking disapprovingly at Jardeen.

Jardeen nodded.

"Long way from home, aren't you?"

Again, Jardeen nodded.

"I suppose you're wondering what I was just doing?" He ran a hand along the smooth surface of his desk.

"No, sir," Jardeen answered. "You were using a computer."

The man was surprised. "You're a Nat child. What do you know of computers?"

"Not much, really. Just what I've read." The man didn't respond. He just kept staring at Jardeen. "I've never actually seen one." More silence. "I...I'm not even sure why you need them...I mean...why not use a pencil?"

"I was under the impression that most Nats, especially children, knew little of technology," he finally said.

"Well...we don't really have any. Except the farm equipment, and we get that from you—the Techs, I mean."

"Then how do you know about computers?" he suddenly shouted.

Jardeen almost fell over with fright.

"I...I read about them," he stammered.

"Where?"

"Ah, in books. The Council of Elders have a small library. Mum talked them into letting me read the books, sometimes. And Tria—"

"What?" bellowed the man. "Tria!"

"Ye...yes. I...I met her in the forest."

The old man suddenly calmed down, his face growing tired. He rubbed a hand across his eyes then spoke again, in a quieter voice.

"I want the whole story," he said. "Why you are here. How you got in and where you met Tria."

✵ ✵ ✵

"What?" Nareen and Gwenna exclaimed.

"Jardeen's been kidnapped," repeated Nala.

"But that's impossible," said Nareen at the same time as Gwenna said, "Who would want to kidnap our son."

"Listen," said Nala. "Did Jardeen tell you where he was the other day?"

"No," said Nareen, looking at his wife. Gwenna shook her head.

"Well, he told me," said Nala. "He went into the pine forest. He went all the way to the end." She paused for effect. "He actually reached the Dividing Wall."

Nareen gasped his surprise.

"And he met a Tech," Nala continued. "He got away, but he told me he might have been followed."

Nareen and Gwenna looked worried.

"Early this morning, I heard noises coming from Jardeen's room. I was half-asleep so I didn't take much notice. Later, I couldn't find Jardeen. When I checked his room, it was a mess. It looked like there had been a struggle."

She paused, staring straight at her parents. "Jardeen has been kidnapped by the Techs, and we've got to do something about it."

✵ ✵ ✵

"An interesting story," said the man." But now I want the truth."

"What do you mean?" asked Jardeen. "That was the truth."

"I don't think so." The man stood up and walked out from behind his desk, slowly.

Jardeen watched the light reflecting from the silver markings on his black uniform.

"I believe you met Tria in the pine forest and I believe you learned how to get in here from her. But that is all I believe. I don't believe you're here to try and join us, as you put it. And I don't believe that you're here without the knowledge of your people."

Jardeen stared at him, dumbfounded.

"Let me tell you what I think," the man finally said, circling around Jardeen. "I think you're here to spy on us. I think you know about computers because you've been briefed by the Nats who put you up to this. I know that there is a rebellion brewing. I know that there are radical elements in the Nat community that aren't satisfied with their lot in life."

Spying? Radical elements? What was this guy on about?

The man stopped in front of him again. Then he bent slightly to bring his face up close to Jardeen's.

"They probably thought that a child would be beyond suspicion." His eyes stared into Jardeen's. "But they were wrong."

He straightened up again. "I want names," he snapped. "Tell me right now. Who put you up to this."

"I don't know what you're talking about—"

The man suddenly yelled. "Do you want to spend the rest of your life in prison?"

✳ ✳ ✳

Nala watched anxiously as the five old men and women shuffled into the Council room. They were unhurried in their movements as they sat down at a rough, wooden table.

Nareen put a hand on his daughter's shoulder when she opened her mouth to speak.

"Patience," he whispered shaking his head.

After what seemed like far too long a wait for Nala, the head of the Council, Saran, cleared his throat.

"We find the evidence to be inconclusive," he announced.

"What?" Nala gasped, only to be silenced by disapproving looks from her parents.

"A number of things may have happened," he continued. "Jardeen may have gone back to the forest of his own accord. He may have run away. He may—"

"But the struggle in his room—"

"Silence," demanded a second Council member.

"We have taken all the evidence into account," Saran continued. "As well as what Nareen, Gwenna and Nala have said." He paused, looking directly at Nala. "You are young and reckless. We cannot and will not take arms against the Techs just because you believe they have kidnapped your brother."

He turned to look at Nareen and Gwenna. "We will wait until this afternoon, in case Jardeen has indeed wandered off into the forest. If he has not returned by then, we will do as you ask and contact the Techs to ask them if they know what happened to him."

Nareen and Gwenna nodded. Nala's temper raged beneath a neutral expression. If the Council isn't going to do anything, she thought, then I will.

✵ ✵ ✵

The man gave Jardeen a shove, and he stumbled into the small bare room. The man then pressed his palm to the wall and metal bars filled the doorway, separating them. "Your new home," he smiled.

"But I haven't done anything," pleaded Jardeen.

"You'll be here until you tell me the truth."

"But—"

"Jardeen!"

That's Tria's voice, thought Jardeen, trying to look down the corridor.

"Are you okay?"

Jardeen nodded with relief. He had never in his life been so happy to see anyone.

"Let him out, Marshal Atrec," Tria demanded.

So it is Atrec, Jardeen thought.

"You're hardly in any position to make demands, Cadet. Especially since you gave this Nat spy the entry code to our part of the ship."

"But he's not a spy," said Tria.

Atrec smiled. "We'll see about that. A few days

without food should loosen his tongue. I'm very interested to hear what he has to say."

"You can't do that!"

"You," said Atrec, pointing a finger at Tria, "are in enough trouble as it is. Don't make it worse." He turned and marched off.

"Don't worry," Tria said to Jardeen. "I'll get you out. I'll go see the commander right now."

🕸 🕸 🕸

"The Council won't do anything," spat Nala.

Her friends exchanged determined looks in the dim light of the old storeroom they used for meetings.

"It's up to us now." Nala narrowed her eyes. "Get everyone together, immediately! And get the weapons."

🕸 🕸 🕸

The door slid open. Tria led Jardeen into a large room filled with people sitting at desks like Marshal Atrec's. Jardeen counted twelve men and women in blue uniforms.

They were all tapping on the surface of their desks, displays hanging in the air in front of them. These displays showed many different things—star charts, complex mathematical equations, planets, and many other things that Jardeen could not even begin to fathom. A thirteenth person sat at a larger desk on a raised area in front of all the others. It was towards this person that Tria led him. Jardeen assumed that she was the commander. Her uniform was a darker blue than the others, with gold markings on the collar and sleeves.

As they approached, she said "Complete," and her display evaporated.

"Commander," said Tria, stopping in front of the raised area.

"Cadet Tria," responded the woman. "Please bring your guest into my office."

Jardeen followed Tria up the three steps leading to the raised area, thinking to himself that this was a very strange office. When they stopped in front of the desk, the commander tapped a finger to her desk and four walls slid up from the floor enclosing the entire raised area. Jardeen tried to hide his surprise.

The commander smiled. "Hello, Tria."

"Hi, Mum," Tria responded.

This time, Jardeen didn't manage to hide his surprise. So that's how she got me out, he thought, glancing at Tria.

She introduced him, "This is Jardeen."

"A pleasure to meet you," said Tria's mother, standing and holding out her hand for Jardeen to shake. "I'm Trianna Lansen, commander of the *Mayflower*."

"The what?" Jardeen asked as he put his bag down and shook her hand.

"The *Mayflower*. It's the name of this ship." She sat back down. "It's named after a famous sailing ship that carried colonists over a wide ocean from one continent to another." Seeing the confusion on Jardeen's face she dismissed the topic. "It all happened a very long time ago on Earth."

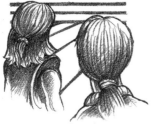

She tapped her desk again and two seats appeared out of the floor. "Please, sit down."

Commander Lansen now looked over at her daughter, her expression hardening a little.

"I've just spoken to Marshal Atrec," she said. "Putting aside the fact that he is furious because you went out into the Nat area, he is convinced that our young visitor here is a spy."

"He's not a—" Tria began, but the commander cut her off.

"He is insisting that Jardeen be imprisoned and questioned further."

"But—"

"Even if he is not a spy, the marshal believes him to be a security risk."

"Ah…" began Jardeen. "What's going to happen to me?"

"Well," said the commander. "If you are a spy, the marshal wants you imprisoned. If you're not a spy, he wants you returned to Nat territory as soon as possible."

"But, Mum…"

The commander held up her hand. "But I am not Marshal Atrec," she said, smiling at Jardeen. "I don't see danger around every corner and I don't look upon the Nats as a threat. I think that a little co-operation is long overdue. I'm sure that we could be more welcoming to our guest."

Tria sighed with relief.

"As for you, young lady," she said, turning her attention back to Tria. "You should not have entered the Nat area. You can consider your leisure privileges suspended." Tria's face fell. "No entertainment holo-vids and no dessert sticks until further notice."

"But—"

"No buts." She turned back to Jardeen. "Now, Tria has told me a little about you already. But I'd like to hear your own story."

🕸 🕸 🕸

"The Council has just decided to send a delegation to the Techs," reported a young man with red hair.

Nala raised her eyebrows. "That could work in our favour. They'll be a distraction."

She and her friends looked back down at the map Nala had stolen from the restricted area of the Council archive. Nala pointed.

"We enter here. My brother told me how to get in, so we shouldn't have any problems." She looked up, her face grim with determination. "But once inside, be prepared to fight."

🕸 🕸 🕸

Jardeen was beginning to get very tired of grey metal corridors. The Tech world seemed to be filled with them, and grey metal rooms with grey metal desks and grey metal chairs. He hadn't been in this new world for one day and he was already missing the colours of the plants and animals of his world.

"So I'm allowed to stay?" asked Jardeen as he and Tria walked down yet another corridor.

"Yeah," she answered. "At least for the time being. Mum'll keep Atrec off our backs."

They walked on for a while in silence.

"So that room back there…" Jardeen began.

"Mum's office?"

"No the bigger room, with all the people working at their desks."

"The Control Centre."

"Ah," said Jardeen, as if he suddenly understood everything. "That's where you control the ship from. So those people fly the ship and look for planets to land on?"

"Don't be silly," Tria laughed. "We don't fly the ship."

Jardeen stopped. "What do you mean?"

"Everything's automatic."

"Huh?"

"The ship flies itself," said Tria. "It's been pre-programmed to navigate and fly and everything. It automatically checks for suitable planets every time we pass a solar system."

"So what were all those people doing?" asked Jardeen.

"They were doing maintenance work," explained Tria in an off-hand manner. "The ship is a very complex piece of technology and we need to make sure that is runs properly. Every circuit, every part of it needs to be checked and double-checked regularly."

"Oh." Jardeen looked very disappointed. In his mind, he had built up this image of the Tech people controlling the ship in a similar way to him riding a bicycle.

"So, is that all your people do?"

"No," Tria answered a little irritably, stopping in front of a door. "We also study and do training in preparation for landing. I'm learning to be a botanist, just like my father. That's why I was in the pine forest. I go there often to identify plants."

Tria pressed her palm to the panel beside the door, and it slid open.

"This is where I live," she said, walking through.

Another room, thought Jardeen as he followed her, just like all the others.

CHAPTER THREE

Two Worlds Collide

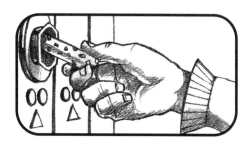

TRIA TOOK A nutrition stick out of a hole in the wall, "And then the food comes out here." She offered it to Jardeen.

He took a bite, but what he really wanted was a salad sandwich or one of his mum's chicken pies.

Jardeen and Tria were seated on stools in Tria's room, beside a smaller version of the desks everyone in the Tech world seemed to have. Jardeen chewed thoughtfully.

"So, if this is your room," he said, swallowing his mouthful, "where do you sleep?"

Tria tapped her desk and a bed slid out

from the far wall. "Right there," she said. With the bed out, the room looked very crowded, indeed. It was much smaller than the room Jardeen had in his parent's house.

"There are shared bathroom facilities," continued Tria. "And I do most of my training right here at my desk as well."

She tapped the desk and a display appeared in the air above it. It showed a forest, on Earth.

"This program allows me to access all sorts of botanical information."

Tria tapped away at her desk as she spoke.

"I like pine trees. They're my favourite sort of plant."

The display zoomed in on a pine tree and then a second display appeared with all sorts of information about its origins, life-cycle, preferred climate, and much more.

"I can have audio as well." The sound of wind blowing through pine trees filled the room. "I can even get the smell."

The scent of pine wafted through the room. "But it's not the same as the real thing." Tria gave the desk one last tap, and the picture, sound and smell disappeared.

"That's why I went into the pine forest."

Jardeen nodded his understanding. While the picture, sound and smell she had shown him was very impressive, it didn't compare to the real thing. Something that Jardeen had in his everyday life. Suddenly, he felt a little sorry for Tria.

"Do you ever get bored?" Jardeen asked, trying to change the subject.

"No. Why?" Tria looked genuinely puzzled at the question.

"Well," said Jardeen, "you seem to have all you need in the one room. Don't you get bored just staying in here all the time?"

"I'm not a prisoner," Tria laughed. "I don't have to stay in my room."

"Yeah, but you sleep in here, you eat in here, you study in here."

"Yes and no," Tria interrupted. "I can eat in here if I want to. Or I can eat in the common room with the other kids."

"Other kids?"

"Well, I'm not the only one, Jardeen,"

said Tria. "I have lots of friends, you know."

"Oh," said Jardeen sheepishly, feeling a little foolish for having assumed Tria was the only person his own age in the Tech world.

"And I do lots of other things outside of my room," she went on. "As well as training to be a botanist, I'm also training to be an officer. I have training with the other cadets."

"You're training to be an officer," Jardeen blurted out. "Wow!"

"Well, Mum is the commander. And her dad was the commander before that. It's kind of expected that I might follow in her footsteps." Tria was looking a little awkward. "But botany is what I really love."

"Like your dad."

"Yes." Tria fingered the disk that hung from her bracelet. "Like my dad."

Tria suddenly looked very sad, silently gazing at the little metal disk. Jardeen let the silence stretch, reluctant to say anything more just in case her change of mood was his fault. Finally, Tria looked up.

"I'm sorry," said Jardeen, "if I upset you."

"It's okay," she answered. "I sometimes feel sad when I think about Dad. He died about a year ago." She looked back down at the disk.

"Oh." Jardeen didn't know what to say.

Tria detached the disk from the bracelet and held it up. An image of a man appeared, floating above it. He was wearing a blue uniform like most of the Techs. He had dark hair and a kind face, but looked a bit strained.

"Your father?"

Tria nodded. "He didn't like having holo-images taken. This is the only one I have."

"He looks like a nice man," said Jardeen in an attempt to say the right thing.

Tria smiled. "He was."

A chime sounded, interrupting them. Commander Lansen's voice said: "Tria. Would you and Jardeen report to Conference Room Two, please?"

Commander Lansen, Marshal Atrec and two other Techs were already there when Tria and Jardeen entered the conference room. The commander introduced Jardeen to Lieutenants Rearden and Noland, who both said "Hello"

and then remained silent for the rest of the meeting. The commander indicated for everyone to sit at the large oval desk.

"It seems we have a problem," she began.

"Please, Commander," Atrec interrupted. "This is more than just a problem. It could disrupt our relations with the Nat Council."

"Marshal," said the commander, raising her voice. "I am well aware of your views on the matter at hand."

Atrec continued, "The Nat child must be expelled immediately. It's the only solution."

"Excuse me," ventured Tria. "We are here, you know. You needn't talk as if we're not."

Atrec was about to reply, but was cut off by the commander.

"Tria, Jardeen, I'm sorry. We really should explain things before going any further." She shot Atrec a frown. "We've had a message from the Nat Council, asking about you."

Jardeen's eyes widened. The Council of Elders, he thought, asking the Techs about me.

"It seems that your family thinks we've kidnapped you."

"But I left them a note," Jardeen explained.

"Be that as it may," Marshal Atrec said,

"they're actually accusing us of kidnapping you."

"Actually," explained the commander, "the Council is not accusing us of anything. They simply inquired as to your whereabouts. It's your parents, and particularly your sister, who think you've been kidnapped. Now, we have informed the Council about what has happened, and they are sending a delegation."

"Hmph," snorted Atrec. "A delegation with weapons, most likely."

"They have agreed not to bring weapons," said the commander, looking sternly at Atrec. "And they will be scanned as they enter." She turned her attention back to Jardeen. "But there is still a problem." She hesitated.

Atrec took the opportunity to dramatically announce, "Rebellion!"

The commander sighed. "The Council say there is some unrest among the younger Nats, and that the story of your kidnapping is making the situation worse."

"What's going to happen?" asked Jardeen.

"That's what we're going to discuss with the Nat delegation. They will be here soon."

"There's nothing to discuss," Atrec insisted. "The boy should be expelled immediately and the delegation should be refused entry." He ignored the commander's expression and continued. "It is obvious that this whole thing is a trick. The boy was sent here by the Nat rebels, assuming we would let our guard down because he is a child. And I'm willing to stake my reputation on the delegation being..."

"Marshal!" warned the commander.

"It's obvious, Commander, that Tria's influence has blinded you in this matter. Your father would not have stood for this."

"Enough!" roared the commander, getting to her feet. "You will keep your theories to yourself, or you'll not be part of discussions."

"Mum and my grandfather didn't always agree about how things should be done," Tria whispered to Jardeen. "There were a lot of arguments when she first took command."

Atrec went red in the face but he remained silent. The commander sat down again.

"My apologies," she said to the others.

"I'm sorry!" Jardeen suddenly burst out.

Every eye in the room focused on him.

"What?" said Tria.

"I'm sorry," Jardeen repeated, lowering his voice. "I just wanted to help find a planet for us to land on. That's why I came here. I had no idea it would cause all this trouble."

The commander's face softened.

"The delegation has arrived," announced an electronic voice suddenly.

"Come in," said the commander, and the door slid open.

Jardeen watched as Councillor Flovia entered. She was the youngest Council member, barely fifty years of age, and the one who had the greatest contact with the Techs, usually leading any delegations that met with them. Nareen, Gwenna and two of the Council attendants followed her. As Flovia moved to greet the commander, Jardeen's parents rushed over to their son, enveloping him in a hug.

The room suddenly exploded with conversation—Gwenna asking if Jardeen was all right; Nareen demanding to know what had happened; Jardeen and Tria both trying to explain everything; the commander welcoming the councillor; while Atrec demanded to know what was happening with the rebellious faction of the Nats. It took several minutes before everyone quietened and sat down. One of the silent lieutenants tapped the table and glasses of water rose up in front of each seated person.

"May we begin," asked Flovia, picking up her glass, "with an explanation from the boy?" Then she took a drink.

"Indeed, we can," said the commander, nodding to Jardeen.

"Ah…well," he began, somewhat embarrassed at having to explain. "I ran away from home to join the Techs."

"What?" his parents chorused in unison.

"Nala insisted you had been kidnapped," his mother went on.

"But I left you a note," insisted Jardeen. "I left it on the kitchen table."

"We never found it," Gwenna assured him.

"And Nala said she heard a struggle," Nareen added. "And when we checked your room, it was a complete disaster—as if someone had taken you by force."

"But…that's impossible." Jardeen looked around, dumbfounded. "There was no struggle.

And I left my room the same as it always is, um, a bit messy, I guess, but not a disaster."

"I don't understand," said Nareen.

"I'm afraid I do," said Gwenna quietly.

"This is why I thought a delegation was in order," said Flovia, "and why I wanted you to come as well."

Understanding dawned on Commander Lansen's face.

"Nala deliberately lied about the kidnapping," continued Flovia.

"But why?" asked Nareen.

"To stir up trouble," Atrec bellowed.

"Nareen," said Gwenna. "You know that Nala has been involved with some of the more radical young people."

"But lying to her own parents?"

"I'm afraid she has done more than that," said Flovia.

They were suddenly interrupted by the same piercing electronic wail Jardeen had heard the first time he entered the Tech area.

"Warning," announced the impassive electronic voice. "Unauthorised personnel have crossed the Dividing Wall. They are armed."

"What?" Atrec rose from his chair.

A lieutenant tapped the table and a display appeared, showing Nala leading a group of young Nats through the Tech corridors.

"Their knives and arrows are no match for our security measures," yelled Atrec. He began tapping at the table in front of him. "They'll be dead before they realise what hit them."

"Wait!" demanded the commander, stopping Atrec, whose finger was poised to start the security system. "Non-lethal measures only."

"But they're attacking us!"

"Non-lethal measures," she repeated calmly.

"I am sorry, Commander," said Atrec, shaking his head. "But as Chief of Security, I have no choice but to override that command."

"No!" screamed Gwenna, as Marshal Atrec lowered his finger.

Jardeen grabbed a glass and threw it at Atrec. It hit him in the arm, splashing water into his face. Atrec roared with anger and the glass smashed to pieces on the floor.

The commander quickly pressed her palm to the table-top and calmly said, "Commander Lansen. Lock down all security systems. Activate only on my orders."

Suddenly the wailing ceased, and the electronic voice spoke again.

✻ ✻ ✻

The computer's voice boomed from one end of the ship to the other. Nats and Techs alike, stopped what they were doing to listen in awe.

"Suitable planet has been located," said the electronic voice. "Repeat. Suitable planet has been located. Estimated time of arrival, ninety-six hours. Repeat. Ninety-six hours."

Waves of excitement, fear and bewilderment washed over the inhabitants of the *Mayflower*. Their journey had finally ended.

CHAPTER FOUR

Recommendations

"**I** THINK I SHOULD be in the exploration party."

Commander Lansen stopped examining the computer scans of the new planet and looked up at her daughter, standing confidently in front of her desk.

"And why do you think that?"

"Because I'm top of the class in botany," Tria said assuredly. "Because our only botanist is too old to be going. And because he thinks I'm the best choice."

The commander raised an eyebrow. "He does, does he?"

"Dr Peterson's recommendation will be in your messages."

Commander Lansen tapped her desk and the scans hanging above the desk were replaced by Dr Peterson's message. She quickly read it and then looked back at her daughter.

"I still think you're too young."

"But—"

"No buts," she interrupted. "There must be someone else who can go."

"There is no-one else," Tria insisted. "Not since Dad died."

Tria instantly regretted having said that. Her mother's face became sad and distant. She misses him so much, thought Tria. Even more than I do.

"I'm sorry..." Tria started to say, but her mother raised a hand to stop her.

"It's okay," she sighed. "I'll think about your request."

✳ ✳ ✳

"The Council have made their decision," said Nareen, looking at his family seated around the dining table. "They have decided that, given the extraordinary circumstances, they won't take any disciplinary action."

Nala breathed a sigh of relief.

"Since no-one was hurt and since there were no actual hostilities, they felt it would be best to leave things at that. They also feel that Nala and her friends were inspired to take the action they did, by the general feeling of mistrust within the community, which the Council takes  responsibility for. Flovia's exact words were: 'We are the leaders. We set the example. We must take the responsibility. We, through our inaction, allowed this to happen.' That is exactly what she said." Nareen paused, he was still trying to take in everything he was relaying to his family. "Since a planet has miraculously been discovered, they think that it is a good time to start afresh in a spirit of cooperation with the Techs."

Jardeen was grinning from ear to ear.

"And that's not all of it," continued Nareen. "The Tech commander has requested the Council to put forward a list of our people they would recommend to be part of the exploration team to go down to the planet."

Nareen paused. "Among the people they have recommended are Nala and Jardeen."

Nala's mouth hung open in surprise. Jardeen could hardly believe his ears, but he jumped to his feet in delight. All his dreams were coming true!

✦ ✦ ✦

"Thank you," Tria grinned.

"For what," asked Jardeen.

"I can go to the planet because of you."

"Huh?" Jardeen was looking confused.

"Mum wasn't going to let me go at first," explained Tria. "She said I was too young. But then when you were picked by your Council, she changed her mind."

"Great!" Now Jardeen smiled.

"How did you get them to pick you?"

"I didn't," he said. "I didn't even ask. They picked me because I always believed we'd find a planet. And because I believed that the Nats and Techs should work together."

"Wow!"

"But I'm not the only strange choice," he continued. "They've also picked Nala."

Tria's eyes widened. "Marshal Atrec won't be happy about that."

"Dad says they picked her because of her courage, and because she acts on what she believes," he shrugged. "He also said something about Councillor Flovia believing in second chances."

"It's going to make for an interesting team," said Tria.

"Yeah," Jardeen nodded slowly.

"Come on, we'd better get to the briefing."

Jardeen brightened up. "Hey! What's the planet called?"

"XB921-457-P31Z."

"You're kidding?"

Tria shook her head.

"It needs a proper name—not just a bunch of numbers and letters," Jardeen insisted. "Something like … like Earth II maybe."

Tria screwed up her face in response.

"Or, um, New Earth."

Tria quickly shook her head.

"Or Eden. Yeah! Eden. After all, it's the start of a whole new world."

Tria nodded her approval. "I like that one."

CHAPTER FIVE

The New World

J ARDEEN LOOKED at the planet they were approaching, through the small round window high up one of the shuttle cabin walls. It looked like a huge blue and green ball. Jardeen was in awe. "Wow!"

"Sit down!" demanded Nala.

Jardeen scowled at his sister as he tore himself away from the view. She returned the scowl when he did a somersault in the air as he floated back to his seat, then did up his belt. Being chosen by the Council to be on the exploration team had changed her. Before leaving, she had apologised to both the Nat

Council and the Tech leaders for her earlier
behaviour—she had even apologised to
Jardeen. Then she had talked a lot about
responsibility. She was definitely bossier.

"She's right," chided Tria. "Stay in your
seat with your seat belt on while travelling in
a shuttle. That's what we were taught in class."

But Jardeen wanted to look out the
window. The view of the planet was breath-
taking. If he couldn't look out the window, he
at least wanted to float around the shuttle
cabin. He had never experienced zero gravity
before. He wanted to have some fun.

Despite his annoyance, he stayed seated
next to Tria, looking around at the six other
occupants of the grey cabin. Apart from him
and Tria, there was Nala, of course, and two
other Nats—Councillor Flovia, and her atten-
dant, Larz.

Then there were the three Techs: Marcus,
a mineralogist; Zara, a zoologist; and Rylan, an
environmental specialist. In the shuttle's cockpit were three more Techs: Farin, the pilot;
Lara, the technician; and Marshal Atrec, who
was in command of the mission.

"Are you excited?" asked Tria suddenly.

"I'm excited." She looked like she was ready to burst. "Very excited!"

Jardeen grinned widely. "So am I."

"We're lucky to be going on this mission. Almost everyone wanted to go."

Jardeen nodded, still not quite believing his luck.

Marshal Atrec's voice then came over the speaker system. "We're about to enter the planet's gravitational field."

Jardeen and Tria grabbed onto their seats, as there was a severe jolt, which accompanied the return of gravity.

"Was that supposed…" Jardeen began.

Another sharp jolt silenced him. The cabin rocked and they heard Atrec say "What the…" before the sound cut off.

Jardeen and Tria looked at each other, eyes wide with fear. The shuttle gave another lurch and the lights flickered. Someone screamed. Panicked voices filled the cabin. The lights snapped off.

The shuttle lurched again and there was another scream. The lights flickered into life briefly. Jardeen looked around at the adults desperately searching for a sign of reassurance.

But there was terror on their faces. Then the lights were gone, the only illumination now coming from the small window.

Suddenly, the pilot said, "Hold on tight. This is going to be a rough landing."

Jardeen felt like he was being shaken apart. He tried hard not to scream. There was one last violent jolt and then all was still. They had landed. No-one said anything. It took quite a while for the shock to wear off.

"Guess you were right about the seat belts," said Jardeen, finally breaking the silence. He grinned at Tria, then they burst out laughing, relieved they were still alive.

"This is no laughing matter," bellowed Nala, which just made Jardeen and Tria laugh even harder.

"That's quite enough," barked Atrec as he made his way into the dim cabin, followed by Farin and Lara. "Is everyone all right?"

There was an assortment of uncertain responses ranging from "maybe" to "I think so." Atrec nodded, then signalled to Lara.

"You may have noticed the somewhat turbulent landing," the technician said nervously. "This was caused by an unexplained loss of power. Farin was able to land the shuttle before the power was completely gone." She paused to look anxiously at Atrec. "However, we are now completely without power. We can't return to or communicate with the ship."

They all silently stared at one another, until Rylan finally asked, "Does that also mean we can't get out of the shuttle?"

"Thankfully," explained Lara, "there is a manual override."

She went over to the external hatch and prised a panel off the wall beside it. She reached in and pulled out a metal handle, sticking one end into a hole beside the panel.

"Someone will need to crank the door open," she said, standing back out of the way.

Atrec pointed to Larz, the largest and strongest of the group. "Make yourself useful."

Larz, dislike for Atrec burning in his eyes, looked to Flovia for instruction. She nodded.

Without a word he got up, pushed past Atrec and started to crank the handle. Soon, they were all standing on the surface of the planet.

Jardeen gasped as he stepped outside. It was everything he had hoped for and yet nothing like what he expected. The sky was the deepest blue he had ever seen. And there was a sun—a magnificent shining orb throwing light and warmth onto everything below. He looked at Tria and was surprised to  see that she looked different. She had a bluish tinge. He looked around at the others. They were all slightly blue. So was everything around them.

"A result of the atmosphere," he heard Rylan explaining to the other Techs.

Jardeen looked up again, marvelling at the sun and the clouds. Puffy, light grey-blue clouds floated across the sky. As they billowed and swirled, they made amazing patterns. Birds, too distant to make out much detail beyond their bright colours, soared in and out of the clouds. From the sky, Jardeen then looked down at the ground. A bluey-green moss grew underfoot. It was soft, spongy and moist. It seemed to undulate under his touch.

There was so much to take in, and all of it so utterly alien. They were in a clear area. There were a few plants a bit further away, with what looked like a forest beyond them in one direction and beautiful purple-peaked mountains in the distance in the other. A tall, thin plant with a gigantic reddish-blue flower caught his attention. Jardeen walked towards it.

"Hold it right there," Atrec demanded. "Where do you think you're going?"

"I'm going to have a look at that flower."

"No you don't," Atrec said, then swung around to address the others. "No-one is to go wandering off on their own. This exploration will be conducted in a disciplined fashion. We will divide into two teams that will go out exploring, with Farin and Lara remaining here to solve our power difficulties."

※ ※ ※

Jardeen noticed it was getting colder. He looked at the other shivering members of his group as they approached the edge of the forest. The sun was hiding behind a bank of clouds. They had put jackets on before setting out, but it was getting colder, with a chill wind that was stronger than anything he had ever felt back on the ship. At least I've seen some weather before, thought Jardeen. He glanced at Tria, teeth chattering as she walked.

Flovia and Larz were at the head of the group, with Jardeen and Tria following, and Rylan bringing up the rear. Jardeen was not surprised when Atrec placed all the Nats in one team and all the Techs in the other. It was only when Flovia objected that Atrec swapped Rylan and Nala. Tria had then insisted that Atrec put her in the same group as Jardeen.

As they came to the outskirts of the forest, Tria rushed forward to examine the trees, Jardeen close behind her. They weren't like anything she had ever seen. They were tall and thin, but without bark and leaves. Every one of them was covered with what looked and felt like fine hairs. The colouring varied from tree to tree—some were bluey-green, some bluey-grey, while others were pure blue. At the foot of some of the trees were what appeared to be mushrooms, and all around, the ground was covered in the same spongy moss. Here and there were large patches of bush-like plants. Jardeen thought they looked like huge tufts of hair sprouting from the moss.

"Isn't this amazing," said Tria, running a hand over the hairs of one tree.

"It is indeed, child," agreed Flovia as she and Larz joined them.

"Oh, I wish the equipment was working," said Tria. "I'd like to get a holo-record of these trees and I want to do a scan."

"I'm sure you'll be able to do that soon," said Rylan, coming up behind them. "We just have to find out what happened to the power."

"Listen," said Jardeen suddenly.

The others quietened and stood still. All around them were the background sounds of a forest—wind whistling through the trees; insects buzzing and humming; the rustle of plants as unseen creatures moved about.

"Nature is rarely silent," Flovia commented before she and Larz started moving on ahead.

"Is it getting colder?" asked Tria, still examining her tree.

"Indeed!" agreed Rylan. "Look at the sky." He pointed to the dark clouds gathering. "I think we're going to have a storm." There was a sparkle in his voice. "Very exciting! I've always wanted to experience weather."

Jardeen noticed that the birds had gone quiet, and felt a niggling sense of dread.

Their attention returned to the ground as they heard a distinct movement among the nearby plants. They all strained to see. Suddenly something shot out of the plants toward them. Tria squealed and started flapping her arms about. Jardeen and Rylan watched in amusement as an insect with bright blue wings zoomed away.

"It's just a bug," Jardeen snorted, ready to move off. Then suddenly he froze, pointing at a hairy, spider-like creature in front of him.

"But Jardeen," Tria mocked, "it's just a little bug."

Rylan laughed as the creature scurried off under a mushroom.

Up ahead, Flovia suddenly raised her hand for silence. As Jardeen, Tria and Rylan quietly

approached, they saw why. A small furry animal was sitting at the base of a tree a few metres ahead. It was about the size of a fox, but with long hind legs like a rabbit. It had small beady eyes, but didn't seem to have any ears. It suddenly jumped from the base of the tree where it had been sitting, to the base of another. They all quietly moved forward.

"Too bad Zara is not with us," whispered Rylan, not taking his eyes off the little creature. "This would be a zoologist's dream."

🕷 🕷 🕷

"The storm is beginning," said Nala, looking up to the sky. "We should turn back."

"Nonsense," sneered Atrec, striding past.

"It could be dangerous," she insisted. "We're not used to uncontrolled weather. You're not used to weather at all."

"I can handle the weather," he snorted. "Can you? Or is the brave Nat too weak?"

They made an odd sight in the alien land-scape, a Nat and a Tech, marching forward, shouting at one another as they went. Neither of them was taking much notice of the wonders around them. It was Zara and Marcus, following at a respectful distance, who were examining the surroundings.

Marcus, a mineralogist, insisted on stopping to examine every outcropping of rock, the strange moss always growing right up to the base. Zara kept stopping to watch the birds. She almost fainted with excitement when a small red and blue bird swooped down to get a better look at them. It was reptilian, with a strange mixture of scales and feathers. It squawked at her, then flew into the gathering clouds. But Atrec and Nala saw nothing.

"Your wonderful technology won't do you any good," Nala was saying, "if there isn't any power to make it go."

Atrec didn't have a chance to retort, for at that moment, the ground beneath them gave way. They scrambled for something to hold on to. But it was no good. All around them, the ground crumbled. And they fell.

✿ ✿ ✿

Flovia and her group were entranced as they followed the little animal to the next tree. At the base was a small bush, thick strands of hair-like vegetation springing from the moss. At the end of each strand was a bright purple berry. Suddenly a long tongue shot out of the tiny creature's mouth and snatched a berry. Apparently satisfied with the taste, the tongue darted out again and again, snatching berries in quick succession.

"Wow!" exclaimed Jardeen.

They then discovered that this creature must have ears. Its head snapped around to face them, then it quickly bounded away, taking huge leaps, much longer than they would have expected for such a small creature.

"Sorry," said Jardeen as the others glared at him. Walking over to examine the bush with Tria, he picked the last of the berries and popped it into his mouth.

"Are you crazy?" snapped Tria. "It could be poisonous!"

"Actually, it's really yummy," said Jardeen. "That little animal was eating it, so I don't think it's poisonous.

"But..." gasped Tria.

"She's quite right," said Flovia, sternly. "It might not be poisonous

to the animal, but it may be to us. That was a very stupid risk."

It was the first time Jardeen had seen Flovia angry. He looked guiltily down at his feet. Any further discussion was halted by the onset of rain—not the fine drizzle that fell every night in the Nat area of their ship, but large, heavy drops.

They all peered into the forest when they heard a faint trumpeting sound. Through the trees, they were able to make out some large animals crashing off through the undergrowth.

"Must be getting out of the rain," said Tria.

"I think we'd better do the same," suggested

Rylan, looking back up at the sky. The clouds now obscured the sun and the wind had risen to a wail. "The storm is starting."

❋ ❋ ❋

As they approached the shuttle through the rain, they saw Marcus running towards them.

"Atrec," he gasped between breaths as he reached them. "And the Nat. Fallen down...into a big hole...got to help them."

Immediately, Flovia started giving orders. "There's rope in my bag back at the shuttle. Jardeen, Tria and Larz—get it and go with Marcus. You can use it to pull them up."

Larz looked at Flovia, obviously unwilling to leave her. "They'll need your strength," she told him. "And you will make better time without me. Don't worry, Rylan can help me back to the shuttle. Now go!"

CHAPTER SIX

Rescue

TREC'S EYES FLICKERED open as he regained consciousness. He was lying down and every part of his body ached. Nala was watching him.

"Are you okay?"

Atrec grunted. He tried to get up, but a stabbing pain shot through his left leg.

"My leg," he gasped. "I think it's broken."

He closed his eyes briefly, taking a deep breath and gritting his teeth against the pain.

"What happened?" he asked, trying to take in his surroundings. They appeared to be in a cavern. A hole at the top showed a stormy sky.

"We fell," explained Nala, pointing up at the hole. "The ground gave way beneath us."

"We've got to get out." Atrec made another attempt to get up, but fell back in pain.

"Try to rest for now," said Nala. "Marcus has gone to get help."

Atrec looked up at the hole in the cavern. Rain was falling through it onto them. They were shielded from the worst of the storm, but could hear it raging above them—the sound of the wind echoing through the cavern.

"You know," said Nala, sitting down next to Atrec. "We're going to have to work together if you want to get out of here."

✦ ✦ ✦

Marcus led Jardeen, Tria and Larz through the storm-swept landscape. The change in weather made everything seem even more strange and unfamiliar. Jardeen had read about storms and other extremes of weather. It was much more violent than he had expected. The rain hammering down at them. The wind roaring like some angry beast. Everything in turmoil.

Eventually, they came to a large patch of ground devoid of the spongy moss. Zara was there, waiting anxiously.

"Thank goodness you made it," she said. "I was afraid that the storm might have stopped you."

They all joined Zara at the edge of moss, and Marcus pointed out to the centre, where a large gaping hole in the ground was visible.

"Marshal Atrec and the Nat were—"

"Her name is Nala," Jardeen interrupted.

"Sorry! Atrec and Nala were at the head of the group, arguing about...something. When we reached this patch of moss-less ground, they just went straight ahead—I don't think they even noticed it. Zara and I stayed back to examine where it stopped—this was the first time we had seen the ground underneath."

They all looked down to see the crumbly, brownish-blue soil.

"I was just about to call out to them, when the ground underneath them collapsed. They fell down into some kind of underground cavern. Atrec is injured. We had no way of getting them out, so I went back for help."

Larz, rope in hand, strode out onto the moss-less ground.

"Wait!" shouted Zara, stopping Larz in his tracks. "Walk slowly and carefully. We don't know how stable the ground is and we can't handle any more injuries."

Larz nodded his understanding and set off again, this time at a more cautious pace. Jardeen and Tria looked at each other, nodded in unison and then headed off after Larz. They joined him at the edge of the hole and peered over. They could see Atrec lying at the bottom of the cavern, with Nala sitting at his side.

"Nala," Jardeen called out over the sound of the storm, leaning closer to the edge.

She looked up. "Jardeen! Get back! It's not safe!"

As if to back up Nala's warning, the ground under Jardeen's feet crumbled. He felt it give way. He started to topple and flailed about in panic. Then suddenly he stopped. Larz had grabbed him by the collar of his overalls. With seemingly little effort, the large man hauled him back to safety.

"Thanks," he gasped, collapsing to the ground.

Larz just nodded and then tossed one end of the rope over the edge.

"Climb up," Tria called, trying not to get too close to the edge.

"No!" Nala shouted back, her voice barely audible over the storm. "Atrec is hurt. I think his leg's broken. You'll have to pull him up."

"Okay. Tie the rope around him and tell us when you're ready."

"Put your arm around me," Nala told Atrec, "and I'll help you up."

Atrec nodded reluctantly. Nala struggled to help him into an upright position. He leaned against a large boulder as she secured the rope around his chest.

"Okay!" Nala yelled.

As Atrec felt the rope go taut, he grasped Nala's arm and looked into her eyes.

"Thank you," he said.

Nala nodded uncertainly. And then he began to rise.

✳ ✳ ✳

Jardeen and Tria hauled at the rope with Larz. The rain made it difficult to grip the rope without slipping. Slowly, they pulled Atrec to the surface. As he appeared over the edge, Atrec scrambled for a handhold but the ground crumbled in his grasp.

"Marcus. Zara," Tria called above the storm. "We need some help."

Marcus rushed forward from the edge of the moss, where he had been watching. Zara took only a few steps, then quickly scurried back like a frightened child.

With Marcus now gripping the rope, Tria signalled to Jardeen and they let go. Sliding over to the edge on their stomachs, they reached out and grabbed hold of Atrec's arms, then they hauled him up. He yelped in pain. Quickly, they dragged him away from the edge. Atrec lay back, gasping, the wind and rain beating down on him. As Larz and Marcus lowered the rope again, and Tria tended to Atrec, Jardeen dashed off into the storm. Tria called out to him, but her words were swept away by the howling wind.

Just as Nala was climbing out of the hole, Jardeen returned with some tree branches.

"What are they for?" Atrec asked weakly.

"To make a stretcher," said Nala, nodding her approval. "Good thinking, Jardeen."

Atrec groaned again, then he passed out.

🕷 🕷 🕷

The force of the rain made walking difficult. Their journey was slowed further by having to carry Atrec on the makeshift stretcher that Jardeen and Nala had constructed from tree branches and rope. By the time they finally made it back to the shuttle, they were tired, muddy, soaked to the skin and frightened. Staggering into the shuttle, they put down the stretcher and collapsed into the seats.

"I didn't think we were going to make it," Zara whimpered.

"You're safe now," Flovia assured, as she quickly examined Atrec's leg.

Each of the travellers started babbling all at once—each trying to relate their story. It was only as Atrec regained consciousness, groaning loudly, that they remembered him. Lara fetched the first-aid kit and found painkillers, bandages and splints.

"Oh no," gasped Tria, while Zara was putting Atrec's leg in a splint.

"What's wrong?" asked Jardeen.

"My holo-disk." She was holding on to her bracelet. "It's gone. It must have come off while we were pulling Atrec out of the hole."

Jardeen looked at Tria. He could see that she was struggling to fight back tears.

"Let's go look for it," he suggested.

"We can't," she sobbed. "It's too dangerous to go out in the storm."

It could get washed down that hole by the rain, Jardeen thought but he did not say anything to Tria.

By now, the painkillers started to kick in and Atrec returned to his old self.

"Farin. Lara," he barked. "The lights are on, so we have power again. What happened?"

"It seems all the power cells have been drained of antimatter," said Farin,

"What's antimatter?" asked Jardeen.

"It's a bit hard to explain," Tria whispered to him, still clutching her bracelet. "It's sort of like the opposite of matter. When antimatter is mixed with matter, it creates energy. That's how we get our power."

"We rigged up a makeshift solar collector," Lara explained. "But with the stormy weather, the power will run out soon."

"Call the ship," demanded Atrec. "Now!"

Farin headed into the cockpit, emerging a few moments later.

"We have contact, sir." He handed Atrec a communications microphone.

"This is Marshal Atrec," he barked. "Let me speak to the commander."

"Lansen, here," came the reply. "No need to shout, Atrec."

"Ah…" Atrec faltered. "Commander, we have a situation. We lost power the moment we entered the atmosphere. Something here is draining the antimatter from the power cells.

"Farin and Lara have set up a solar collector, but the power's not going to last much longer. I suggest you do another scan of the planet, with the specific intent of finding the source of the power drain."

The lights began to flicker.

"Will do!" Commander Lansen's voice was barely audible over the static. Everyone leaned in closer to Atrec, trying to hear. At that moment, someone opened the door to the outside, letting in a blast of cold wind and rain.

"Shut the door," yelled Atrec, but whoever had opened it, had closed it again.

"Is there anything else…" The power cut out and the commander's voice disappeared.

"Damn," spat Atrec as they were plunged into darkness.

There were a few minutes of chaos as people fumbled about and started talking all at once. Soon their eyes became accustomed to the dim light seeping in through the window.

"Jardeen's gone," Tria suddenly cried.

CHAPTER SEVEN

Eye of the Storm

TRIA WAS TRYING desperately to squeeze through the barely opened door. As Marcus attempted to pull her back inside, the storm lashed at her from outside.

"Come back in here, at once," she heard Atrec bellow from within.

Tria kept struggling. Jardeen had gone into the storm to find her holo-disk. She couldn't leave him out there on his own. She squirmed out of Marcus's grip. He made another grab for her, but missed, and she lunged forward.

Finally outside, she faltered as the full force of the storm hit her. *I must be mad,* she thought. But she didn't look back. She just ran in the direction she knew Jardeen had gone. The clouds were so dark and the rain so heavy that she could barely see. The wind lashed at her, trying to push her back.

Suddenly, there was a huge booming sound, so loud that Tria couldn't hear her own scream. She threw herself to the ground, covering her head with her hands. Moments later, she looked up. In the distance, the sky blazed with blue light as a huge ball of fire came streaking down, exploding on impact with the ground.

At first she thought she was under attack—that the rightful owners of the planet were returning to drive them away. It was several minutes before her terror subsided enough for her to remember watching a holo-vid about lightning. Tria forced herself to get up. She had to go on.

Thunder boomed again. The sky blazed. For a moment, as another ball of fire streaked across the sky, she thought she saw a figure in the distance. It had to be Jardeen.

"Jardeen," she yelled at the top of her lungs, but the wind whisked her voice away.

She began to run. She kept screaming Jardeen's name, even though she knew he would not be able to hear her. Thunder boomed for a third time and the sky lit up.

"Jardeen!"

It was him. He was running towards her.

Suddenly Tria stopped. She stared helplessly as a fireball of lightning hurtled down from the sky towards Jardeen. The whole thing seemed to happen in slow motion. Jardeen also stopped running. He looked up into the sky. Tria could imagine the look of terror on his face as he saw the approaching fireball.

It didn't hit Jardeen, instead it crashed straight into a tree nearby. Jardeen dived out of the way as the huge tree exploded into flames. From where she stood, Tria saw branches fly out in all directions, one headed for Jardeen.

"Watch out!" she yelled.

Jardeen looked up to see the large branch crashing down on him.

Tria screamed and starting running. The storm no longer mattered. Her tears mixed with the rain as she reached Jardeen's still form, lying pinned under the branch. There was a gash on his forehead and blood running down his face.

"Oh, please don't be dead." Tria fell to her knees, patting his cheek.

Jardeen didn't respond.

"Jardeen," she wailed, shaking him. "Wake up. You've got to wake up..."

Tria dissolved into sobs, still shaking him.

Suddenly he groaned and his eyes fluttered.

"You're alive!" she yelled.

"Yeah," moaned Jardeen. "And I've got something for you."

He lifted his arm and opened his hand. Sitting on his palm was Tria's holo-disk, the image of her father spinning above it.

"I didn't know how to switch it off." He smiled wanly, then winced with pain.

Tria's tears suddenly turned into laughter. She took the disk, switched it off and hugged him as he lay in the mud. Above them the thunder crashed yet again, the sky blazed and another fireball exploded in the distance.

"We'd better get out of here," said Tria.

Jardeen raised a hand to his temple and touched his wound. Then he tried to pull himself out from under the branch. Gasping with pain, he slumped back.

"I'm stuck," he said, raising himself up and trying again. "I can't get out." Jardeen looked desperate as he struggled against the weight. "It's pinning my legs down."

Tria jumped to her feet and grabbed the branch, heaving at it. It shifted slightly and Jardeen tried again.

"You need to lift it higher," he said.

"I can't," gasped Tria as the branch slipped out of her hand. "I'm not strong enough."

"Come on. You have to try again."

With rain pouring down around her, Tria shifted her feet, trying to get a better foothold on the slippery moss. She grabbed the branch and heaved. It shifted a little, but Tria slipped and went crashing down beside Jardeen.

"It's no good. I can't do it by myself," she sobbed.

Suddenly everything stopped. The rain, the wind, the storm—they all ceased. Jardeen and Tria were bathed in sunshine.

"Huh?" Jardeen looked up into a circular patch of blue sky, dark clouds swirling angrily around it.

Tria got to her feet and looked around. Not far from them, on all sides, the storm continued to rage.

"We're in the centre," she marvelled. "We're in the eye of the storm!"

"We'd better get a move on while we've got the chance," Jardeen reminded her. "If I sort of sit up like this, I can get a grip on the branch. Come on. Let's try this together."

"Okay." She grabbed the branch again. "Ready?"

Jardeen nodded and together they threw all their energy into lifting the branch. Slowly, it began to shift.

"Almost there," Jardeen puffed through gritted teeth. "Just a little bit more."

As the branch came up a little more, Jardeen kicked and slid out from underneath.

The branch came crashing down again, just as the eye of the storm passed. Slowly, Jardeen got to his feet and limped a few steps.

"Are you okay?" asked Tria.

He nodded, smiling despite the pain, his face plastered in mud and blood.

"Thanks!" he said, as the storm raged around them again.

"Thank you!" said Tria holding up her holo-disk, her face also covered in mud.

They both laughed and hugged each other.

CHAPTER EIGHT

A New Home

JARDEEN AND TRIA stood in the observation area that overlooked the shuttle bay. Technicians were doing final checks on the shuttles and people were loading stuff on board.

"Hard to believe," mused Jardeen.

"What?" asked Tria. "That we're colonising the planet?"

"I mean, Nats and Techs working together." He pointed down to a Tech who was helping Jardeen's father load chickens aboard one of the shuttles. "Three weeks ago, I would have said it was impossible."

Tria grinned. "A lot's happened since then."

Jardeen nodded. He looked down at the row of shuttles, waiting to transport people, equipment, plants and animals to the surface of their new home. He thought they looked odd—their sleek grey forms now lumbered with gold solar panels that just didn't look like they belonged. Solar power was going to be their main source of energy.

The commander had looked somewhat baffled as she had tried to explain it to him.

"The planet's core is made of some sort of…um…it's not matter, but it's not anti-matter either. We're not sure what it is. But it's producing a field of some sort, around the planet, which turns antimatter into matter."

So the Techs had got to work converting everything to solar power.

"Attention please." Commander Lansen's voice jolted Jardeen out of his thoughts. "I would like to announce that a new Council, made up of Nats and Techs, has been set up to oversee the colonisation. Its first decision has been to name the planet Eden."

Jardeen looked at Tria in surprise.

She grinned back and shrugged. "I just passed on your suggestion to Mum."

Epilogue

"...and so, it is now my great pleasure to officially open the festivities for the twentieth anniversary of Landing."

Jardeen and Tria were holding hands as they stood with the rest of the crowd in the Town Square of Foundation City. The Council Head's long speech ended and people began to move off.

"Not too boring for you?" Jardeen asked Myra, who had been standing next to him and his wife.

"No. It was okay, Dad." The young girl shrugged. "But what are Techs and what are Nats?"

Jardeen smiled at Tria, then looked down at their daughter. "Now that is a long story..."